To Jeff,

Great Thoughts Of All Time

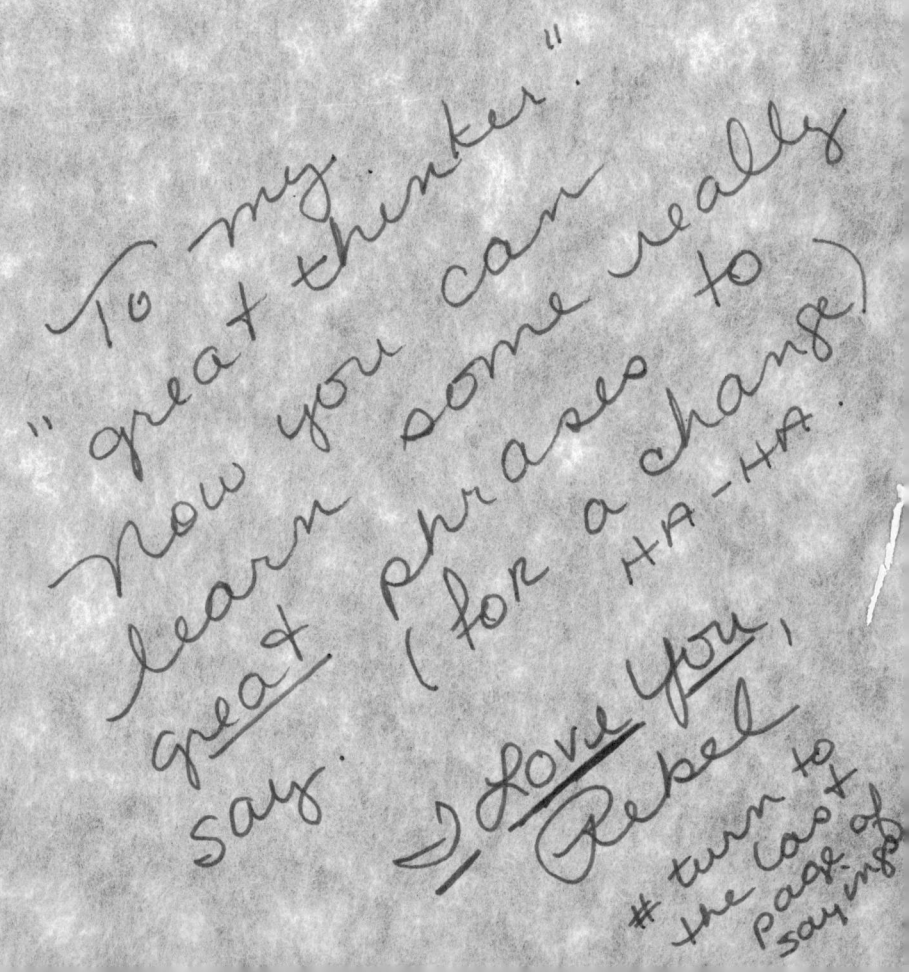

To my "great thinker": now you can learn some really great phrases (for a change) to say. HA-HA.

I Love you,
Rebel

turn to the last page of sayings

ROBERT KOLBRENNER

Great Thoughts Of All Time

Selected By Dean Walley

April Editions™

Copyright © 1973 by April House, Inc. All Rights Reserved.
Printed in the United States of America.

Great Thoughts Of All Time

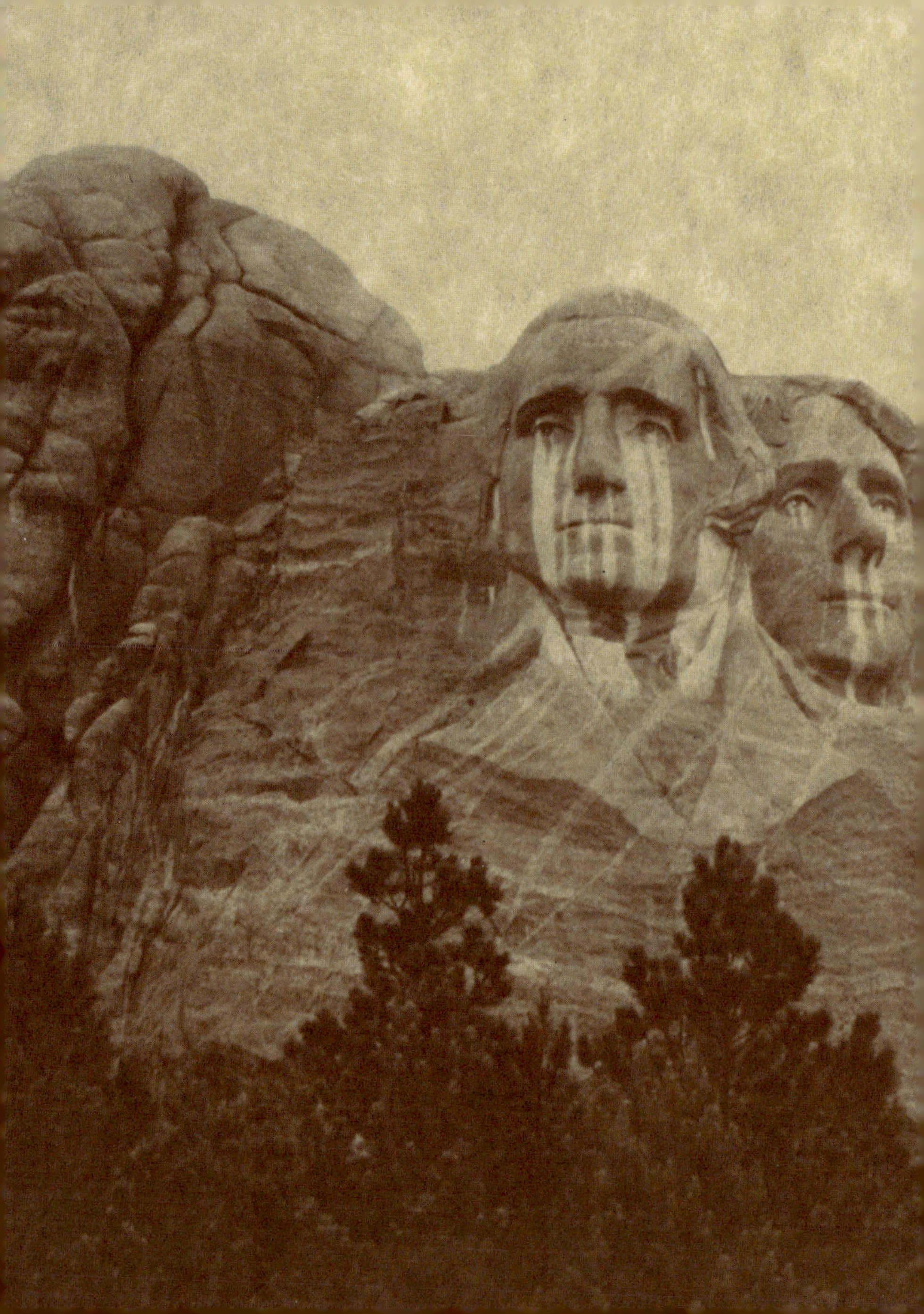

What man's mind can create, man's character can control.

THOMAS EDISON

BRUCE PINE

There are two tragedies in life. One is to lose your heart's desire. The other is to gain it.

> GEORGE BERNARD SHAW

An easy task becomes difficult when you do it with reluctance.

> TERENCE

Pain and effort are not just symptoms which can be removed without changing life…they are rather the modes in which life itself, together with the necessity to which it is bound, makes itself felt.

> HANNAH ARENDT

The measure of a man's life is the well spending of it, and not the length.

PLUTARCH

TORY DUNTLEY

JAMES FROMME

Let us make haste to live, since every day to a wise man is a new life.

SENECA

Remember this—that very little is needed to make a happy life.

MARCUS AURELIUS

Fine art is that in which the hand, the head, and the heart…go together.

JOHN RUSKIN

To write simply is as difficult as to be good.

SOMERSET MAUGHAM

To be of use in the world is the only way to be happy.

HANS CHRISTIAN ANDERSEN

ROBERT KOLBRENNER

The world is a looking glass, and gives back to every man the reflection of his own face.

WILLIAM MAKEPEACE THACKERY

We must love our friends for their sake rather than our own.

CHARLOTTE BRONTË

If a man could mount to Heaven and survey the mighty universe, his admiration of its beauties would be much diminished unless he had someone to share in his pleasure.

CICERO

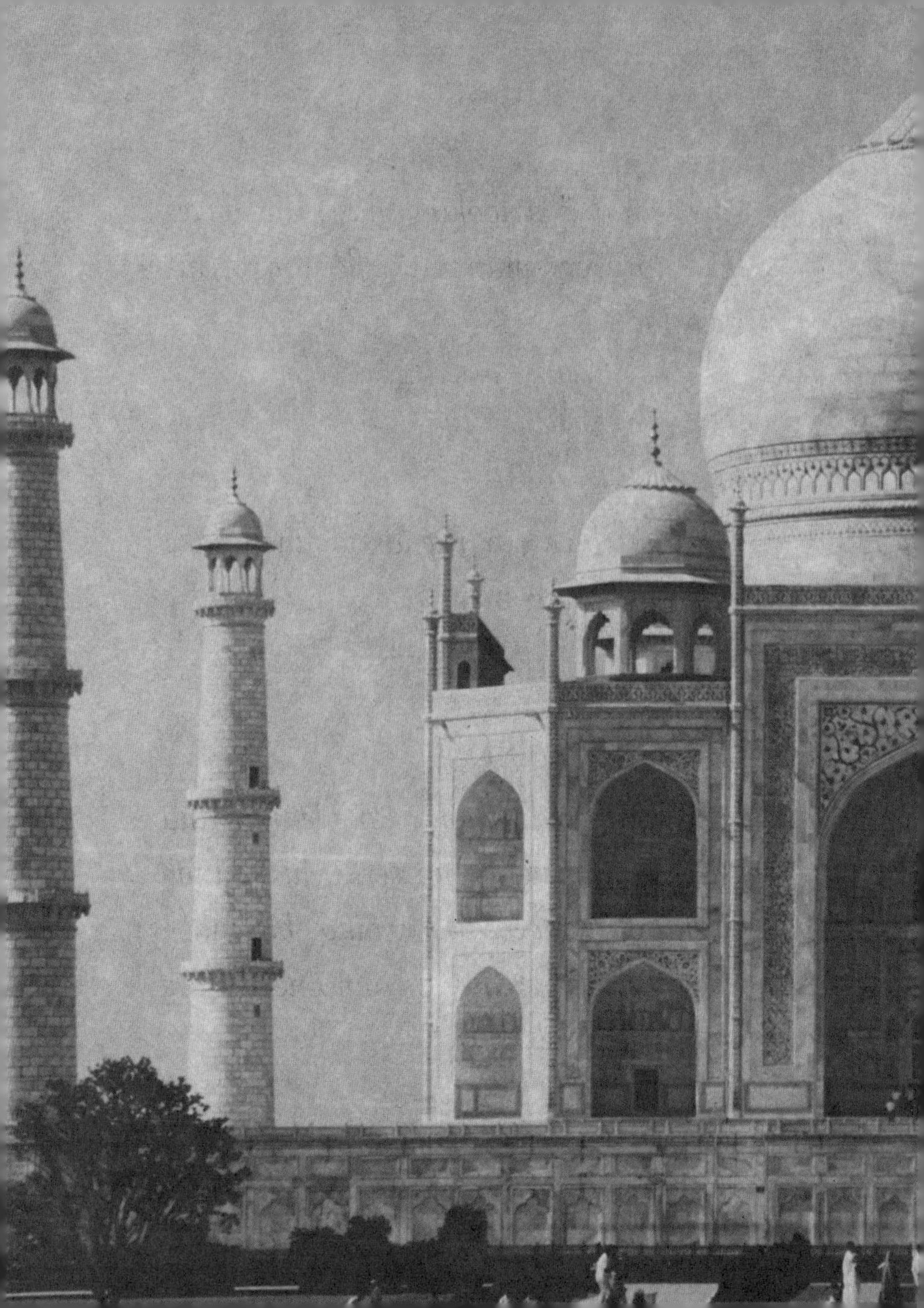

NORMAN N. ROYALL

Nature never breaks her own laws.

LEONARDO DA VINCI

One hour of life, crowded to the full with glorious action, and filled with noble risks, is worth whole years of those mean observances of petty decorum, in which men steal through existence, like sluggish waters through a marsh, without either honor or observation.

SIR WALTER SCOTT

Everything has been thought of before, but the difficulty is to think of it again.

GOETHE

A man should not strive to eliminate his complexes but to get into accord with them: they are legitimately what directs his conduct in the world.

SIGMUND FREUD

Fanaticism consists in redoubling your effort when you have forgotten your aim.

SANTAYANA

A man should never be ashamed to own he has been in the wrong, which is but saying in other words that he is wiser today than he was yesterday.

ALEXANDER POPE

MIKE McCLUE

What is happiness except the simple harmony between a man and the life he leads?

ALBERT CAMUS

A thing of beauty is a joy forever: its loveliness increases; it will never pass into nothingness.

JOHN KEATS

When truth is buried underground it grows, it chokes, it gathers such an explosive force that on the day it bursts out, it blows up everything with it.

EMILE ZOLA

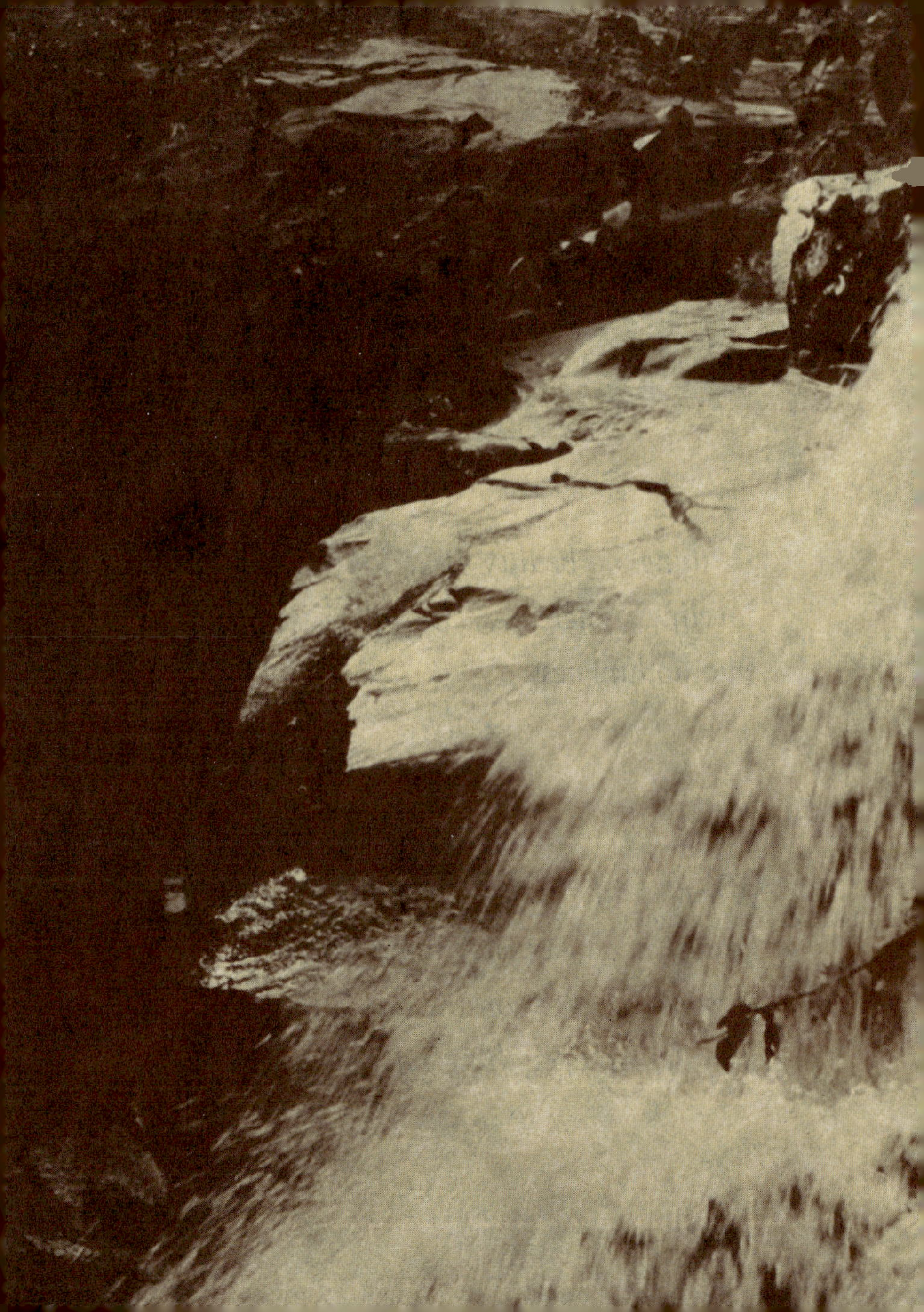

LEROY PREUDHOMME

I have immortal longings in me.

WILLIAM SHAKESPEARE

To live in the presence of great truths and eternal laws—that is what keeps a man patient when the world ignores him and calm and unspoiled when the world praises him.

HONORÉ DE BALZAC

As one grows older one is more impatient with subterfuges and shams generally, and increasingly desirous that the "last run" at least should be free from them.

JANE ADDAMS

Fear to do base, unworthy things is valor; if they be done to us, to suffer them is valor too.

BEN JONSON

LEROY PREUDHOMME

TED WOODARD

No race can prosper till it learns that there is as much dignity in tilling a field as in writing a poem.

BOOKER T. WASHINGTON

It is never any good dwelling on goodbyes. It is not the being together that it prolongs, it is the parting.

ELIZABETH BIBESCO

Perched on the loftiest throne in the world, we are still sitting on our own behind.

MONTAIGNE

Let no man think lightly of good, saying in his heart, "It will not benefit me." Even by the falling of waterdrops a water pot is filled; the wise man becomes full of good, even if he gathers it little by little.

BUDDHA

LEROY PREUDHOMME

To be great is to be misunderstood.

RALPH WALDO EMERSON

Death destroys a man, but the idea of death saves him.

E. M. FORSTER

One does not love a place the less for having suffered in it.

JANE AUSTEN

The cheerful live longest in life, and after it, in our regards.

BOVEE

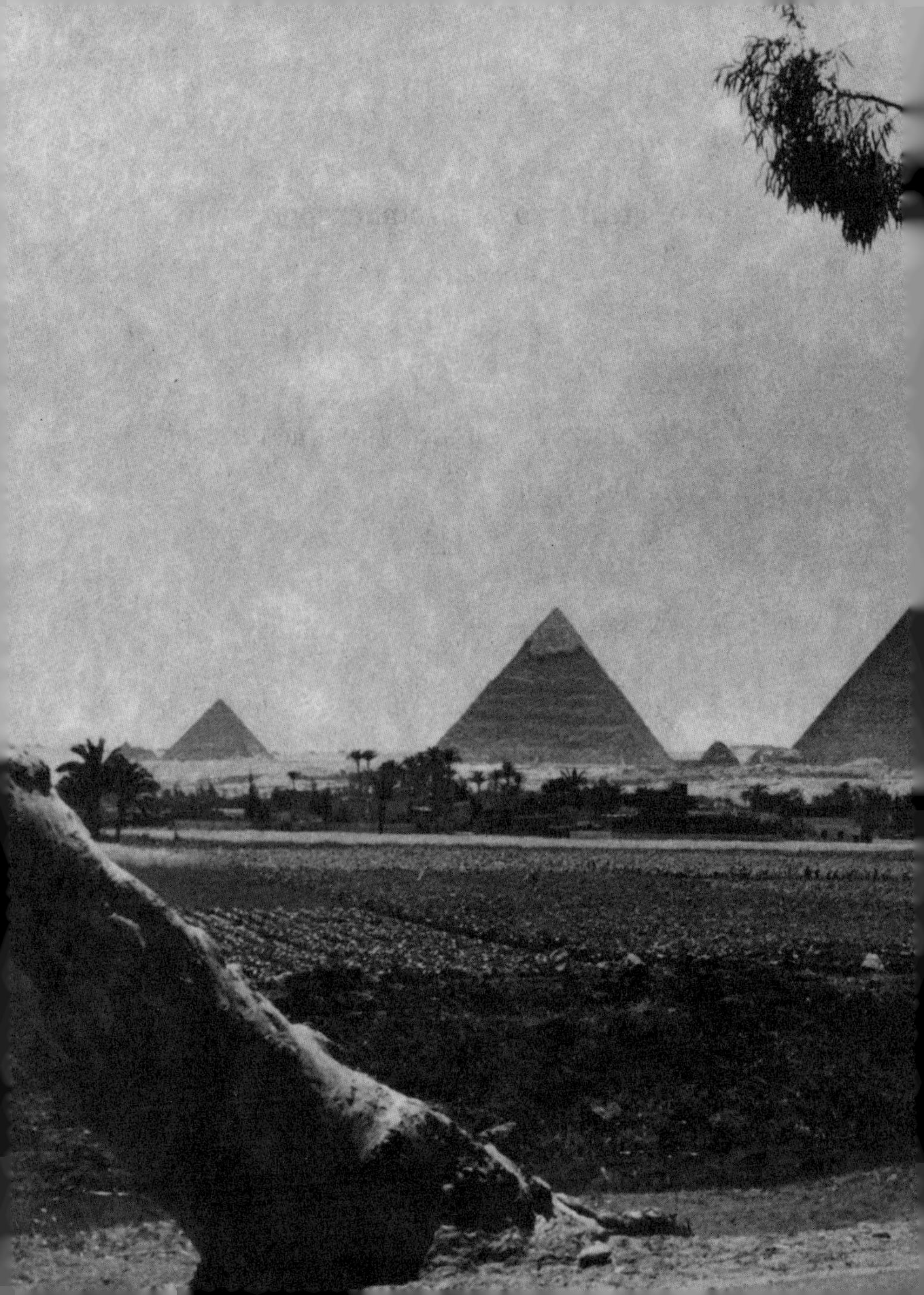

NORMAN N. ROYALL

Men are more ready to offend one who wishes to be beloved than one who wishes to be feared.

MACHIAVELLI

To be what we are, and to become what we are capable of becoming, is the only end of life.

SPINOZA

Hope is both the earliest and the most indispensable virtue....If life is to be sustained, hope must remain, even where confidence is wounded, trust impaired.

ERIK ERIKSON

For love and beauty and delight, there is no death nor change.

PERCY BYSSHE SHELLEY

He is a hard man who is only just, and a sad one who is only wise.

VOLTAIRE

It is well to think well; it is divine to act well.

HORACE MANN

The only rose without thorns is friendship.

MLLE. DE SCUDERY

JAMES LIPP

Take time to deliberate; but when the time for action arrives, stop thinking and go in.

ANDREW JACKSON

The only conquests which are permanent, and leave no regret, are our conquests over ourselves.

NAPOLEON

Truth is the beginning of every good thing, both in heaven and on earth; and he who would be blessed and happy should be from the first a partaker of the truth.

PLATO

To have doubted one's own first principles is the mark of a civilized man.

OLIVER WENDELL HOLMES, JR.

A forgiveness ought to be like a cancelled note, torn in two and burned up, so that it can never be shown against the man.

HENRY WARD BEECHER

If a man does not keep pace with his companions, perhaps it is because he hears a different drummer. Let him step to the music which he hears, however measured or far away.

HENRY DAVID THOREAU

There is virtue in country houses, in gardens and orchards, in fields, streams and groves, in rustic recreations and plain manners that neither cities nor universities enjoy.

AMOS BRONSON ALCOTT

LEROY PREUDHOMME

LEROY PREUDHOMME

The highest possible stage in moral culture is when we recognize that we ought to control our thoughts.

CHARLES DARWIN

The more we love our friends, the less we flatter them.

MOLIÈRE

No man is rich enough to buy back his past.

OSCAR WILDE

Common sense is very uncommon.

HORACE GREELEY

The first forty years of life give us the text; the next thirty supply the commentary.

SCHOPENHAUER

They are able because they think they are able.

VIRGIL

It is good to love in a moderate degree, but it is not good to love to distraction.

PLAUTUS

Every man is like the company he keeps.

EURIPIDES

In cases of difficulty and when hopes are small, the boldest counsels are the safest.

LIVY

Women have served all these centuries as looking glasses possessing the power of reflecting the figure of man at twice its natural size.

VIRGINIA WOOLF

To every thing there is a season, and a time to every purpose under the heaven.

ECCLESIASTES 3:1

To know what you prefer, instead of humbly saying Amen to what the world tells you you ought to prefer, is to have kept your soul alive.

ROBERT LOUIS STEVENSON

LEROY PREUDHOMME

One should take good care not to grow too wise for so great a pleasure of life as laughter.

JOSEPH ADDISON

Whoever degrades another degrades me, and whatever is done or said returns at last to me.

WALT WHITMAN

Happiness makes up in height for what it lacks in length.

ROBERT FROST

On the mountains of truth you can never climb in vain: either you will reach a point higher up today, or you will be training your powers so that you will be able to climb higher tomorrow.

NIETZSCHE

Nothing is so wholesome, nothing does so much for people's looks, as a little interchange of the small coin of benevolence.

RUFFINI

Let mystery have its place in you; do not be always turning up your whole soil with the ploughshare of self-examination, but leave a little fallow corner in your heart ready for any seed the wind may bring, and reserve a nook of shadow for the passing bird; keep a place in your heart for the unexpected guest, an altar for the unknown God.

AMIEL

Love is the great Asker.

D.H. LAWRENCE

STEVE McCONNELL

It is much better to be envied than pitied.

HERODOTUS

Compassion is the chief law of human existence.

DOSTOYEVSKY

Imagination is more powerful than knowledge.

ALBERT EINSTEIN

Be slow to fall into friendship; but when thou art in, continue firm and constant.

SOCRATES

See, honey; when I'm quiet I'm thinking about "our moments"!

There are many moments in friendship, <u>as in love</u>, when silence is beyond words.

OUIDA

True bravery is shown by performing, without witnesses, what one might be capable of doing before all the world.

LA ROCHEFOUCAULD

There is a certain relief in change, even though it be from bad to worse; as I have found in traveling in a stage coach, that it is often a comfort to shift one's position and be bruised in a new place.

WASHINGTON IRVING

Set in Goudy Oldstyle.
Printed on Roman Parchment.
Designed by Pamela Luehrs Roski.